Pearls Within the Storm

The Words Inside the Music

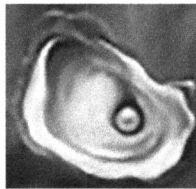

Kamaya Productions
www.amyhindman.com
amy@amyhindman.com ~ kamaya1717@gmail.com

Pearls Within the Storm
The Words Inside the Music

Printed in the United States of America

All content written and recorded by:
Amy Hindman / Kamaya Productions
Book Design and Editors: Amy Hindman
Kaylan Daane and Susanne Romo
Creative Consultants: Julie Stamper and Kaylan Daane
Cover Painting: Mary Sparrow, Fiverr Angel: Eswarik K.
http://www.marysparrow.com
CD Cover Art: Anne Martin McCool
http://www.annemartinmccool.com
Library of Congress Cataloging-in-Publication Data
Hindman, Amy
   Pearls Within the Storm
   The Words Inside the Music
   I. Authorship I. Title

ISBN: 978-0-9996971-0-8 (paperback) black & white
ISBN: 978-0-9996971-1-5 (ebook) color
Library of Congress Control # 2018960651

Thanks for purchasing my book!

Free Gift!

To get your free mp3 of my

original song

Livin' in the Let Go

Please go to:

http://www.amyhindman.com/contact.html

About the Author

Amy Hindman is an award-winning songwriter whose songs have won placements in the 2012, 2013, 2016 and 2018 International *Song of the Year* Songwriting Competition, with judges including Paul McCartney, Sting and Rihanna. This worldwide competition is based solely on songwriting abilities. Amy's song *Gandhi* and *King: Becoming the Dream* received an "Honorable Mention" and was endorsed by Arun Gandhi, the grandson of Mahatma Gandhi.

Amy's song *Puget Symphony* took first place in the NW Songwriting Contest. She is a performing artist, singer, and guitarist and has recorded three albums of original music. She sang with Academy Award winner and renowned folk singer Burl Ives on the stage performance of *On the Old Front Porch*, and has performed her original music at Seattle's Bumbershoot Festival.

Amy is a published author whose chapter *Loss of Innocence* is in the Anthology *Life Sparks: Life Stories to Illuminate, Inspire and Ignite* Volume I. The story is her account of living through a turbulent time of loss for the United States, with the death of President John F. Kennedy, as well as the death of her mother.

She received a Bachelor of Arts Degree in English and American Studies from Whitworth College in Spokane, Washington.

Much love and appreciation to Kaylan,
for her uplifting spirit of love and adventure.
As we continue to spiral up into greater and
greater versions of ourselves and our
extraordinary lives, we are truly being who
we were birthed to be.

Table of Contents

Kamaya Productions

Amy Hindman CD's:

Beneath the Surface	©® 1992
Beyond the Edge	©® 2000
In My Waking Dream	©® 2013

Books:

Life Sparks

Life Stories to Illuminate, Inspire and Ignite

© 2016 Luminare Press

Amy
Hindman

Beneath
the
Surface

Beneath the Surface CD 1992

Journey to the Soul / Beneath the Surface

Puget Symphony

Solo

Bertha Wilhelmina

Prayer for my Child

Deep Therapy

The Gift (for Karleen)

Gentle Friend (Wendysong)

Shakti Moondance

Mystery

Journey to the Soul / Beneath the Surface

Inspiration

I moved to a little log cabin

on Guemes Island in Washington State

after leaving my husband and partner of ten years.

This was part of my journey through the

dark night of the soul, and it became

my ultimate freedom ~ truly coming into my own.

Journey to the Soul / Beneath the Surface

The Song ~ December 1991

On this journey letting go of control

guide me, guide me so I know

passage through the darkness to be whole

illuminating hidden shadows I disown

Whimpering voices demanding to be heard

denied for so long orphaned in this world

conditioned in survival severed from the whole

On this journey letting go of control

guide me, guide me so I know

Beyond the Illusion beneath the surface so much more

embracing the duality surrendering to my soul

guide me, guide me so I know

guide me, guide me so I know

Puget Symphony

Inspiration

I was inspired to write this song when I was walking home
from a party at three AM and saw the moon setting
on the Skagit Bay. I lived in a 1948 Trotwood trailer
covered with cedar shingles. It had a wood stove,
a skylight, and leaded glass windows overlooking
the beautiful Skagit Bay. I had never camped as a child,
and this beautiful space was the ultimate joy for me.
This was my home.

Puget Symphony

The Song ~ Summer 1980

Moonset Skagit Bay

sparklin' golden to the Milky Way

think I'm gonna delay my stay

til the clouds disappear it away

Red houseboat circles around

rockin' to the beat of the sound

Whidbey lights come a flickerin' through

its windows like a haunting guru

Soothing Puget Symphony

gently rockin' me away to the sea

moonset sinkin' through a clouded veil

intoxicating moonlight ale

Pairs of lovers greetin' the sea
sharin' in its mystery
rowboat dancin' by the red houseboat
lovers makin' moon a la float

Soothing Puget Symphony

gently rockin' me away to the sea

moonset sinkin' through a clouded veil

intoxicating moonlight ale

Mornin' comes rollin' around
rowboat lies still on the ground
tide wanes out, ocean lullaby nil
but rockin' with a harmony still

Moonset Skagit Bay
Moonset, moonset Skagit Bay . . .
Moonset Skagit Bay

Solo

Inspiration

My 1948 Trotwood trailer

When this song was written,

I was living on Pull and Be Damned Road

outside of La Conner, Washington.

I was in my late twenties, feeling very alone.

Solo

The Song ~ Summer 1980

Restless times for love
and wishin' I could sleep beside a man
that's not like all the others
not just casual intimacy

Strangers in a strange land indeed
who are you who is me
and why can't we come together
we're fillin' a void that only gets wider
acting as if we both really care
yet still I'm sittin' here today
watchin' the sun play on the bay

Alone at home

just a pen and my thoughts

high tide singin' strong

fire's cracklin', lanterns low

wish I had a beau

just someone to share with

just to be there with, to hold me when I'm low

Strangers in a strange land indeed

who are you who is me

and why can't we come together

we're fillin' a void that only gets wider

acting as if we both really care

yet still I'm sittin' here today

watchin' the sun play on the bay

Bertha Wilhelmina

Inspiration

I awakened one morning when I was twenty-eight, sobbing because my mother had died seventeen years ago. I was stunned to realize that this pain was still there after so many years. I wrote this song when I was in therapy, feeling the grief and loss that had never really been addressed.

I remember my mother saying to me, "whatever you do, *don't* name your kids after me!"

Bertha Wilhelmina

The Song ~ July 1988

I remember when you told me

"Don't name your kids after me"

but that would leave a great big hole

in the family tree

it's really not such an atrocious name

when I remember your soft gentle face

my mother is who you are

and Bertha Wilhelmina is pearls covered with lace

And you're still so much a part of me

it's from you I got my identity

though you weren't there to show me how to be

I can feel your spirit move, movin' through me

Don't ya wish somehow
we could've altered that untimely fate
seems amazin' that my heart
didn't just fill up with hate

Losin' you so long ago, it still wounds me so
now I'm just lettin' it bleed
healin' with the help of your love
the wounded child in me

And you're still so much a part of me
it's from you I got my identity
though you weren't there to show me how to be
I can feel your spirit move, movin' through me

I never knew I looked so like you

you left me as a little girl

became a woman I wish you knew

photographs of you yesterday, I resemble today

the essence of your beauty

will sparkle within me always

And you're still so much a part of me

it's from you I got my identity

though you weren't there to show me how to be

I can feel your spirit move, movin' through me

I can feel your spirit move, movin' through me

Prayer for My Child

Inspiration

This song, I imagined, would have been my mother's response to the wounded part of me.

Amy with Mom ~ Davenport, Iowa

Prayer for My Child
The Song ~ July 1988

My brave little one

your pain is almost done

soon you will be dancing in the sun

the journey you are moving through

becoming the love that was given you

letting the pain overflow

discovering what you didn't know

freeing your life from the shadow

melting into the beauty of the rainbow

You know that I can feel your pain

wounded child cryin' in the rain

though I've been gone for all of these years

I have always dried your tears

for I am always near, feeling all your fear

just call on me, my little one, I am here

My youngest little prize, "bonus baby"* of five

you've walked through the storm with your head up high

remembering the words to our lullaby

so go ahead and let yourself cry

I'm so sorry I never said goodbye

leaving my Amy, my little child,

wondering why

You know that I can feel your pain

wounded child cryin' in the rain

though I've been gone for all of these years

I have always dried your tears

for I am always near, feeling all your fear

just call on me, my little one, I am here

My sweet child, I can still feel you smile

your serenade of love still touches me

soothing like a rhapsody

listen carefully for my reply

I come to you through dream and lullaby

"When at night I go to sleep

fourteen angels watch do keep" **

My brave little one, your pain is almost done

soon you will be shining like the sun

living in the light we are one

My mom and dad always referred to me as their "bonus baby"*

**from Humperdinck's *Prayer from Hansel and Gretel*

Deep Therapy

Inspiration

In the midst of my therapy, I was struggling
and trying to understand exactly what I had been
through with the loss of my mother, and how it had
affected my life today.

Deep Therapy

The Song ~ March 1989

First day of spring

wish I knew what I was feeling

my mind needs clearing

Like a closet filled with webs of darkness

ghosts fade in and out of focus

pain and fear locked somewhere in my mind

the child remembers it somehow

please trust my journey through you now

together we'll expose the lurking shadows

and tenderly our love will light the way

Somehow I just need to sing

take the time to be listening

the wound keeps bleeding patiently

revealing unknown mystery . . .

searchin' for the key inside of me

Memories buried long ago

photographs refuse to share the story

there was no glory when you let go

left alone you took the map

and no one else could fill the gap

and all that rage I turned it in on me

and now I just want to be free

First day of spring

wish I knew what I was feeling

The Gift (for Karleen)

Inspiration

This was written when I was feeling immense
gratitude for my therapist. With her help,
I was able to heal the wounds of my childhood
by expressing with her, what was unexpressed
with my mother.
I emerged whole, knowing this scar would always
be a part of me, but it no longer had to define me.

The Gift (for Karleen)

The Song ~ March 1990

I wonder if you see the gift that you've given me

the courage to grieve

as you led me through forgotten memory

Guiding my hand

facing ghosts of long ago buried in this wasteland

the journey she denied

the tears we should've cried

the love laid down and died

withdrawn long before it was time . . . such a crime

now here you are giving to me

all that she couldn't be

She never said goodbye

the children didn't ask why

but when in bed alone they'd cry

prayin' that she wouldn't have to die

Guiding my hand

facing ghosts of long ago buried in this wasteland

the journey she denied

the tears we should've cried

the love laid down and died

withdrawn long before it was time . . . such a crime

now here you are giving to me

all that she couldn't be

I wonder if you see the gift that you've give me

the power to be free

by listenin' to the wounded child in me

being my friend, knowing on you I can depend

the rage no more denied

suppressed feelings now brought into the light

creating a space open wide

where sleeping dreams no longer hide

thank God I'm alive ...

I wonder if you see the gift that you've given me

Gentle Friend (Wendysong)

Inspiration

Wendy is my dear friend, soul sister and mentor.

She was there for me at a time of tremendous

grief, and she is a shining light in my life.

We have shed many tears, and experienced

much joy and laughter;

I am so blessed to have her in my life.

Gentle Friend (Wendysong)

The Song ~ July 1988

Gentle friend, I'll be with you til the end, and then ...
if you get there before I do
try to remember what we've been through
please touch me now and then
with tender loving care
for I'd miss the warmth of your body
from way out there

I know when loved ones die
no one ever leaves
but our bodies are a treasure we receive
and the language of love through your body flow
lifts me when I'm feelin' low
your loving touch releases me to flow

You've seen my pain, and I've seen plenty of yours

we've shed our tears as loved ones come and go

we've cried and laughed and sighed

at times we wanted to die

sometimes we with eagles soared

and other times wondered why

we signed up for the course

I know when loved ones die

no one ever leaves

but our bodies are a treasure we receive

and the language of love through your body flow

lifts me when I'm feelin' low

your loving touch releases me to flow

Gentle friend, I'll be with you til the end, and then ...

If you get there before I do

try to remember what we've been through

please touch me now and then

with tender loving care

for I'd miss the warmth of your body

from way out there . . .

for I'd miss the warmth of your body

from way out there . . .

Shakti Moondance

Inspiration

I wrote this song a month before I left
my relationship of ten years.
I had outgrown my former self and had
to expand my life as I knew it.
Shakti Moondance allowed me to create
a vision of who I was to become.

Shakti Moondance

The Song ~ September 1991

And now I know it's time to let go ...

the dying moon mirrors the dance my body knows

the shedding of the old

reflects the pain within my soul

healing passage through the dark will lead me home

healing passage through the dark to be reborn

and the mystery cycle begins anew

New moon, the light will return real soon

New moon sometimes inspires a tune

Magic moon, mysterious rune

Guru moon, please guide me to my shadow

through the darkness

where the Goddess lies in slumber deep

Awaken her dormant power in me . . .

New moon, the light will return real soon

New moon, sometimes inspires a tune

Magic moon, mysterious rune

Magic moon, mysterious rune

magic moon   magic moon

Mystery

Inspiration

This song came to me when I was in the sacred pool at Breitenbush Hot Springs in Oregon. I had wanted to go to Breitenbush for many years, and I was finally able to go.

I truly felt that I was immersed in the womb of the earth, and received much healing in these sacred surroundings.

Mystery

The Song ~ October 1992

Healing waters, healing waters of the earth

cleansing waters, cleansing waters of the earth

Stones of mystery, here long ago before me

Earth history speaks to me

Sacred pool envelop me

womb of the earth replenishing ~ let it be . . .

Welcome the mystery

wisdom of the Mother Earth guiding me

gathering strength ~ emerging free

Sing of earth's melody, joining in life's harmony

Breitenbush River symphony

healing me ~ healing me

Amy at Breitenbush Hot Springs ~ Oregon

BEYOND THE EDGE

Amy Hindman

Beyond the Edge CD 2000

Sweet Sorrow

Give Yourself to Love
(Kate Wolf) lyrics not included

Beyond the Edge

A Self Outworn

In a Lifetime (For Kaylan)

Changed

Once

Livin' in the Let Go

Magic Island Lullaby

Beyond the Mists of Avalon

Star Child

Spirit of the Deer

Sweet Sorrow

Inspiration

After living alone for six years

in my beautiful log cabin on Guemes Island in

Washington State, my Soul was guiding me

to leave my sacred home and enter

the next chapter of my life.

Sweet Sorrow

The Song ~ 2000

Feels like it's time to move on
sweet sorrow parting, as I linger on
blessed home, gifting my soul
with her song for so long
sweet shelter from the storm
made my broken heart strong ...

And now I must go out again
and follow the passion of this dream, my friend
and where my heart is leading me now
can't say that I know
so I'll just let go
be the river and flow

And faith has brought me here before

trust in the process an opening door

shedding an outworn self

growing to become more

with the power of love guiding me

my dreams will soar

And now I must go out again

and follow the passion of this dream, my friend

and where my heart is leading me now

can't say that I know

so I'll just let go

be the river and flow

The river is constantly changing, I know

it's not in her nature, resisting the flow

swift current clear water

she travels along she is free

reflecting the truth of my nature,

who I'm birthed to be ~ Being free

Beyond the Edge

Inspiration

When my life was expanding into uncharted territory,

I was challenged in who I believed myself to be.

I had been asking for a partner who shared my vision

of living fully and growing spiritually.

When a woman showed up instead of a man,

I was thinking "whaaaa?"

I had to trust my Soul and a bigger idea.

This song emerged, causing me to stretch beyond

my limited idea of myself.

Beyond the Edge

The Song ~ March 1996

As we journey beyond the edge

identities shift and boundaries fade

exploding voodoo mask promenade

lives redefined in this masquerade

becoming the love that we are

illumination like a shining star

Trust in the magic the heart speaks of

be here now, for I am love

no separation no need to fear

expanding beyond old ideas held dear

stretching beyond who we think we are

trusting in a greater love far beyond

small mind conception

Dancing the edge surrendering all

risking and daring to meet this high call

Problems dissolve when small mind surrenders

guided by love ~ only one mind we're of

Courage it takes to live in faith

seeing beyond the illusions we make

in Truth we create a Sacred Space

Guided by the light we all are one

and every heart we touch embraces all, hear the call

Follow the light within your soul

the gift that we are already whole

in the Silence you'll be your Divinity ~ Ahhhhh

A Self Outworn

Inspiration

I was living on Guemes Island, alone again, when I wrote this song. It had been five years since I left the relationship.

I was growing spiritually, and yet what I call the "Legacy of Loss" was a tremendous source of sadness and grief for me. It was a familiar feeling, having experienced the loss of a loved one at a very young age. Now, though, I was an adult, and had chosen to leave; I was not left. Still, the love never died, and I had to come to terms with letting go of the pain of that loss, with the help of my Spirit Guides and Teachers.

A Self Outworn

The Song ~ November 1996

I used to feel that I belonged to a family
with my man, part of a clan
but now somehow I've outgrown the form
shattered images of a self outworn
suspended somewhere between here and there

Life is a process of learning to let go
or struggling, suffering through another show
the Buddhists say attachment
is the cause of all sorrow
so I pray that I may with all my soul
perfect the art of letting go

The more I grow I leave behind
dear loved ones that I know
the love still felt deep within my soul
leaving is painful, this I know
yet I have many new seeds to sow

Here within this empty space . . .

formless, floating, scared without a trace

direction uncertain, path unknown

with the faith of a child ~ I will be shown

Shiva, the Lord of the Dance ...

the Hindus say he reminds to let go

of that which binds, that we hold onto

what within me must die

so I may fully live

Life is a process of learning to let go

or struggling, suffering through another show

the Buddhists say attachment

is the cause of all sorrow

so I pray that I may with all my soul

perfect the art of letting go

In a Lifetime (For Kaylan)

Inspiration

I wrote this song on Kaylan's birthday, expressing my
love and gratitude for her and who she had become
in my life. My spiritual growth with her was what I had
dreamed of sharing with a partner.

She truly is a pearl amidst the storm. I never
expected my soulmate to come in this package.

In a Lifetime (For Kaylan)

The Song ~ May 2000

In a lifetime we sometimes find
precious pearls amidst the storm, in which we're born
blessing our journey on the way back home
remembering who we're birthed to be, you and me
and together we discover we are free

And the vision that we hold
will keep us young and bold
and our love will fuel the flame
and light our way again
through the mind fields that threaten peace
allowing fear to remain
but now the power of love will guide us home again

Within the mind field there is a shield

that severs love protecting all that we feel

repeating familiar dramas of the child inside

from a time when there was nowhere to run and hide

but now the power of love will guide us home again

And the vision that we hold

will keep us young and bold

and our love will fuel the flame,

and light our way again

through the mind fields that threaten peace

allowing fear to remain

but now the power of love will guide us home again

and the power of love will guide us home again

Changed

Inspiration

I had just spent some time with my father in Texas, who was dying of pancreatic cancer. He listened to my first album, *Beneath the Surface,* in his hospital room, telling everyone who entered how beautiful my songs were, and that they should really sit down and listen to the words. My dad was always a huge fan of my music and writing.

Amy with her dad ~ Davenport, Iowa

1955 Christmas letter

"Our favorite saying of hers is
'Daddy, I'm glad you live at my house.'"

Changed (revised)

The Song ~ September 1998

Today it seems I've changed

somehow the world doesn't feel the same

Familiar shadows revealed again

Sweet sorrows remembering when

And it's strange how the body knows

hidden beneath scarlet ribbons and bows

are wounds of long ago ~ somehow it knows

And now I see through my eyes

what you might see in a different light

loved ones gathered by your side

in the blink of an eye you might die

Walking the ledge to eternity

afraid of dying and leaving your family

on this final journey ~ coming home to be free

The times I've lived in pain, I'd like to go home again

the suffering of this human form

sometimes I wish I'd never been born

Remembering our divinity

obscured within humanity is a life purpose to be free

being who we're birthed to be

I dreamed of you one night

from heaven I came on a ten-speed bike

you were young, so handsome then

My father to be way back when

I knew your face, I loved your smile

but I would not be born for awhile

You didn't know that girl in the hall

she picked her father

cause he was the best choice of all

for creating her path on earth ~ chosen at birth

And daddy you have blessed me

with the presence of love all my life

you've given me so purely

a strength of spirit through strife

So blessings on your journey home

I know for you you'll never be alone

and when you see the light

we'll hold you in flight

Today it seems I've changed

Once

Inspiration

After I had left my husband, I was living alone on
Guemes Island when this song was written.
I was reflecting on my life and who I had become
in that relationship. I had grown immensely with him,
and knew that he was a necessary part of my
journey. I loved and trusted him.
He offered me safe passage through the storms of a
very difficult time in my life, as I worked through the
healing of my mother's death when I was a child.
I began to discover who I was becoming, beyond the
wounds of my past.

Once

The Song ~ June 1993

Once you were my lover

and once my very best friend

on this journey my chosen companion

and once we vowed to share

in the nurturing of our love

from season to season, guided from above

And once you were my hearth and home

sweet shelter from the storm

loving soulmate, spiritual friend

but our path that we had known

had to come to an end, my friend

For the way of the heart is hard and steep

not for those afraid to take the leap into the deep

allowing the storm through the unknown

on this long night's journey home

Through the slow passage of time I mourn

heart aching and forlorn

wishin' that we weren't torn

And now I know that you weren't strong

you needed to remain safe all along

but oh our love could've become

a most beautiful song

For the way of the heart is hard and steep

not for those afraid to take the leap

into the deep, allowing the storm

through the unknown

on this long night's journey home

"Now I lay me down to sleep

I pray thee Lord my soul to keep" *

Livin' in the Let Go

Inspiration

I lived aboard a 32' Nordic Tug in Seattle

on Lake Union for a few months.

I was feeling down one day until I sat on *Lil' Boat*

with my guitar, writing and feeling the rocking

of the boat on the water.

Livin' in the Let Go
The Song ~ Summer 2000

Livin' in the let go

cause I don't really have to know

what's so is so

Lift myself from gettin' low down

chop wood, carry water and row oh oh oh

Got to roll me outta my bed

cause thoughts keep movin' through my head

of things that need to be said

Lil' Boat rockin' and soothin' my soul

takin' me deep into my core

and I know that I am so much more

so much more ~ I soar

Take the time to go within

and realize that there's only one thing

Being . . .

the sense of separation you feel isn't real

Livin' in the let go

cause I don't really have to know

what's so is so

Let go ~ be the water and flow

the wizard lives within you know you know

Let go ~ be the water and flow

the answers lie within you know you know

let go ~ you know . . .

Magic Island Lullaby

Inspiration

I wrote this song at sunset while cruising

on a boat named *Avalon.* We were in MacKaye

Harbor, off of Lopez Island in the San Juan Islands

of Washington State.

Magic Island Lullaby

The Song ~ August 1997

Such a brilliant color like passion lights up the sky

reflecting on the water as another day goes by

magic island lullaby

And *Avalon* will rock you to sleep

safely anchored your Spirit she'll keep

just close your eyes and listen

to the sweet sea melody

while the moonlight's shinin' in the sky

guardian of light

magic island lullaby

And out here where the water meets the sky
all your worries will pass you by
and up on high the winged ones sing and fly
just another magic island lullaby

Through the oceans of the earth
Humpback whales and Orcas at sea
blissfully they breach and dance with their family
and oh, what a wondrous sight to see
the blessings of the earth surrounding me

And out here where the water meets the sky
all your worries will pass you by
and up on high the winged ones sing and fly
just another magic island lullaby

and oh, what a wondrous sight to see
the blessings of the earth surrounding me
the blessings of the earth surrounding me

Amy on the boat *Avalon*

Lake Union, Seattle

Beyond the Mists of Avalon
Inspiration

Kaylan and I took *Lil' Boat*, a 32' Nordic Tug,

out to Orcas Island in the San Juan Islands

of Washington state for the first time,

piloting and navigating ourselves. We went to

Rosario Resort, and tied to a buoy in Cascade Bay.

We completely lost track of time. When we

discovered we had been there seven days, we

couldn't believe it, as it felt like we had been there

for only three.

Beyond the Mists of Avalon
The Song ~ August 1997

It seems we're out here in the middle of nowhere

but we're really somewhere

in the pitch of night she asked

"Are there any boats around us?"

"Yes," I replied,

"Oh, that's good," she said with a sigh.

And through the portside window

boat silhouettes rock and sway

anchored securely come what may

and points of view keep shifting

as we swing in Cascade Bay

we're gaining insight along the way

And I always wanted to be anchored at bay

just floating on the summer sea

rockin' to the rhythm, you and me

and sometimes we don't know

quite where we're goin' to

just cruisin' the blue until we're through

Rosario lit up like Camelot

visioning who we're birthed to be

we're Guardians of the Mystery ~ Keepers of the Key

creating our own destiny, becoming who we'll be

revealing sacred secrets as we drift here out at sea

And though at times it seems to be

uncharted territory, feeling confused and lost at sea

not in control of our destiny ~ but if you look closely

into the eyes of another soul, there are wise ones

of old, Beholders of Wisdom, this I know

"And what's your magic?" a monk once asked me

and my friend, The Keeper of the Keys replied,

as she looked into my eyes

"Your magic, Little Big Heart,

is you hold one truth in song for all to hear

you see there are many points of view

and the center is you ~ your divine nature

is anchoring you

So hold this truth so others can see

that they too are free, we're not alone on this journey

expand your vision far, be the truth of who you are."

And when the earth walk's done

beyond the illusion we're one

and we'll meet beyond the Mists of Avalon

cause we're Guardians of the Mystery

drifting out at sea

Star Child

Inspiration

I was feeling confused and troubled about my life.
My trusted friend, Eileen, who was a psychic, said
she saw me moving to California. I said "California? I
don't wanna move to California!"*
I went down to the beach where I lived on the Skagit
Bay, and tried to make sense of this information.
As I allowed myself to get beyond my head, I was
able to feel the beauty all around me.

After I wrote this song, Eileen said "See Cookie,
you *heal* yourself with your music."

*Turns out, I *did* move to California thirty-three years later.

Star Child
The Song ~ 1980

The sanctuary beyond old messages and lives

the here and now of puppies playin',

Northwestern beaches of slimy rocks

and changing tides

of swaying forceful simplicity

Flowing with the sacred dance

shunning objective realities

buildin' bridges to my soul

Just give me the warm energy of the sun

the salt of the sea

the serenity of knowing we are one in this Mystery

awaken the star child in me

The adventure of changes the fear of the unknown

the child peers into the chasm and weeps

cleanse me with the sea

free me from the boundaries of my mind

echoing all that is Divine

Just give me the warm energy of the sun

the salt of the sea

the serenity of knowing we are one in this Mystery

awaken the star child in me

Spirit of the Deer

Inspiration

I was on the front porch of my log cabin on Guemes Island, staring at a deer about six feet from where I was standing. I grabbed my guitar and created this song as I sang to the deer.

Spirit of the Deer

The Song ~ Guemes Island, WA 1993

Spirit of love ~ spirit of love

spirit of love penetrates all fear

Spirit of love ~ spirit of love

I can feel your healing presence

in the gentleness of the deer

as she lingers near to me free of fear

perhaps the mesmerizing mystical tune

unites us here

trusting in the language of love we both can hear

Spirit of love ~ spirit of love

spirit of love penetrates all fear

spirit of love ~ spirit of love ~ Spirit of the Deer

spirit of love ~ spirit of love

In My Waking Dream
Amy Hindman

In My Waking Dream CD 2013

Puget Symphony (page 14)

The Water is Wide (lyrics not included)

A Kalaloch Song

Seattle Blues / Island Hues

In My Waking Dream

Why the Sufi's Whirl (lyrics not included)

Song of the Earth

Gandhi and King: Becoming the Dream

Summer of My Dreams (lyrics not included)

Tonight You Belong to Me (lyrics not included)

Twinkle, Twinkle Little Star

A Kalaloch Song

Inspiration

My husband and I went to Kalaloch Lodge
on the Olympic Peninsula in Washington State
on our sixth wedding anniversary. This song was
created there, overlooking the Pacific Ocean.
I wrote the last verse a year later, after leaving
the relationship.

A Kalaloch Song
The Song ~ October 1990

Mesmerized by the sea

with its ever constant pounding symphony

Destruction Island signaling light to see

for travelers of the ocean's mystery

While we create a Kalaloch song

celebrate our love as we grow strong

from a tinker toy log cabin by the sea

nine years we've been together, you and me

Sometimes like ships we pass in the night

wonderin' how again we'll see the light

lost within the darkness of the storm

through the fog the dawn will guide us safely home

While we create a Kalaloch song
celebrate our love as we grow strong
from a tinker toy log cabin by the sea
ten years we've been together, you and me

Two Roads still diverged in a purple wood
and still I wanna take you with me if I only could
weary heart and soul keep beckoning me to let go
perhaps my love cannot be contained anymore

And we can hold the *Kalaloch Song*
celebrate our love as we move on
becoming who we are truly meant to be
and the guiding light of love will set us free
and the guiding light of love will set us free

Seattle Blues / Island Hues

Inspiration

I worked for a while in Seattle, while

living aboard The Nordic Tug on Lake Union.

I love visiting the city, but I am not a city girl.

When I was able to drive to my island home

near La Conner in the Skagit Valley, it was

always wonderful to be in the country again

on Fidalgo Island.

Seattle Blues / Island Hues
The Song ~ July 1996

Now I don't know about this work thing

I just wanna sing

I mean this is what I love to do

sing whether I'm happy or blue

gotta get back on track ~ I want my life back

Hyperactive energy of the city weighin' down on me

meter maid keeps on ticketin' me

wanna park my car wherever I be

meter maid quit hasselin' me

Just take me back to the country

in the country I'm breathin' free

slowin' down ~ bein' me

And yes I know it appears to be

that this is a song about the city

but it's really about all the parts of me

city and country inside of me

Within me lies peace and serenity ~ the country

conflict is only in the mind that's not free

it's not the city

And I've received the blessings too

knowin' the joy of bein' with you

rockin' on the water as the sky turns blue

discoverin' what we love to do

Finding our way ~ creating each day

vocation must be for me a passion play

Now some they work for their monthly pay

just enough to get by from day to day

soul suffocating in an endless way

as the clock ticks by dreams decay

I wanna live in a meaningful way

revealin' my soul through work and play

feelin' the wonder of each new day

touching each other in a loving way

For we are so much more

than the small lives we bargain for

when you wish upon a star

you'll discover who you really are

When you wish upon a star . . .

In My Waking Dream

Inspiration

When I awakened from this dream, I was able
to articulate my thoughts and feelings
concerning the ending of my relationship
with my husband.

I had a hard time coming to terms with having
to leave someone I loved so deeply.
What do you do with the love that is still felt,
even though the relationship is no longer working?
Like, where does the love go?

In My Waking Dream
The Song ~ July 1997

I dreamed of you again last night

reunited with family everything felt right

there was no separation in time

coming home to you felt so fine

at a time when your home was mine

And I don't know sometimes what to do

with our love it keeps shining through

the head tells the heart all the reasons we part

still my heart knows there must be a place

maybe far beyond time and space

for our love surrounded in grace

In my waking dream I know we are through
parting then was the best thing to do
cause there was more to life than me and you
the spirit of my dream was dying too
I'd completed my walk with you

And I don't know sometimes what to do
with our love it keeps shining through
the head tells the heart all the reasons we part
still my heart knows there must be a place
maybe far beyond time and space
for our love surrounded in grace

I know sometimes that the choices we make

life decisions on the path we must take

the wisdom of the soul leading us to be whole

may require that the tender heart break

yet the loving heart doesn't seem to know

that there's such a thing as letting go

And I don't know sometimes what to do

with our love it keeps shining through

the head tells the heart all the reasons we part

still my heart knows there must be a place

maybe far beyond time and space …

for our love surrounded in grace

There are no mistakes ~ surrounded in grace

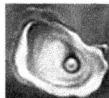

Song of the Earth

Inspiration

Living on Guemes Island, I had been reading
the work of Jamie Sams and was so inspired by
her books, *Medicine Cards*, and *The 13 Original
Clan Mothers*.

I was feeling tremendous gratitude for the animals
as my teachers. This song was written for them,
Honoring the Earth and our Elders who have
come before us.

Song of the Earth
The Song ~ 1995

Out of the earth I sing for them

Out of the earth I sing for them

Eagle spirit soaring in the wind

out of the earth illumination

The Deer, gentleness penetrates all fear

out of the earth ~ healing here

Song of the earth manna of life

Spirit manifest in light

Spirit of life I sing for you

Spirit of life I sing for you

Hawk, magic messenger of the sky

circle my dreams teach me to fly

Ancient voices echo through the night

Honored Elders, guide us in our plight

For we are the Elders now

it's up to us somehow

to remember who we are ~ awaken and bow

Gandhi, Gautama, Jesus the Christ

Beings of Light I sing for them

Ancient voices echo through the night

guiding my soul remembering flight

For we are the Elders now ~ it's up to us somehow

to remember who we are ~ awaken and bow

Oh Great Spirit, may I walk my talk,

Heart open, my Sacred Vow

For we are the Elders now ~ it's up to us somehow

to look within, the answer's always been

Here and Now

Out of the earth I sing for them

Out of the earth I sing for them

Gandhi and King: Becoming the Dream
Inspiration

I wrote this song during the annual

Gandhi King Season for Non-Violence in 2007.

It is a 64-day campaign, spanning the

January 30th and April 4th memorial anniversaries

of Mahatma Gandhi and Dr. Martin Luther King Jr.

For more information:

http://www.agnt.org/season-for-nonviolence

Gandhi and King: Becoming the Dream

The Song ~ 1/30/07

Today marks the season again
to remember the voices of Gandhi and King
non-violence is the theme
and becoming the change in the world we wish to see
becoming it you and me ~ becoming it you and me

Cause it's an inside job to be free
in the midst of confusion, pain, apathy
Love is the power to enlighten me
beyond small mind, it's the key

Got to open my mind wide ~ open my heart wide
allowin' it all in ~ free from judgment,
fear and separation
Being Compassion and Light

Mahatma Gandhi, he believed

that the only devils in this world we see

are those runnin' rampant in humanity

creating a nightmare it seems . . .

an eye for an eye makes the world blind

"Injustice anywhere

is a threat to justice everywhere"*

And Martin Luther King had a dream

that one day all would be free

that all races be joined hand in hand

and see the power of peace throughout the land

*Martin Luther King Jr.

"We shall overcome we shall overcome

we shall overcome some day

oh deep in my heart I do believe

that we shall overcome some day" **

Got to open our minds wide ~ open our hearts wide

Becoming the change, the vision we wish to see

Becoming it, you and me

Becoming it, you and me

**Became an International Song for Human Rights

Twinkle, Twinkle Little Star
Inspiration

I have always loved this song.

I was inspired to write my experience

of seeing my first falling star at my grandparents'

home in Burgettstown, Pennsylvania when I was

about five years old.

Twinkle, Twinkle Little Star
The Song
Amy Hindman Variation

Twinkle, twinkle little star,

how I wonder what you are

up above the world so high,

like a diamond in the sky

twinkle, twinkle, little star,

how I wonder what you are!

When I first saw a falling star

I was at my grandpa and grandma's house

my bed was in the top bunk way, way upstairs

I could hear my grandpa's slippers

shuffling down the stairs

Twinkle, twinkle little star

how I wonder what you are

Staring out the window before I closed my eyes

I saw a brilliant starlight vanish in the sky

amazing to see such a lovely sight,

in wonder I kept staring long into the night

Twinkle, twinkle little star

how I wonder what you are

When you wish upon a star

know in wonder who you are

"Starlight star bright first star I see tonight" *

*Anonymous

MORE CD'S TO COME!

In the near future, I will be releasing my fourth CD titled *Moon of Listening Woman.*

I'm sharing the lyrics to a song I wrote on my 52nd birthday, which will be on the new album. I was living on Fir Island in Washington State and had made plans to meet with friends in Bellingham for a birthday dinner. It was snowing, the roads had gotten dicey, and those plans had to be cancelled. So, I drove down to the gas station, bought two Hostess cupcakes and 24 candles. Why 24? There is no way I could've gotten 52 candles on 2 cupcakes. I went home with Martha, my black cocker spaniel, sang *Happy Birthday* to myself, blew out the candles and wrote my first song ever on my birthday. I am so grateful for my birth and for my life.

The Splendor of Life
The Song ~ 1/15/2005

Fifty-two years ago from today

I was born a minister's daughter

on a cold day in January

my mom and dad said they planned

on a family of four,

and then I made my entrance and said

"How about just one more?"

Born in the Midwest land of the Iowa corn

my brothers and sisters we lived all over the world

my parents they gave of their love

to those men far away

who were serving in wars

that would only lead to their grave

we made them our own, so far from their home

And there's love and compassion everywhere I go

through illusions of sorrow and pain

I somehow know

and sometimes when I wonder

just why I've been born

I know that love has something to do

with my path on earth

My mother wasn't around when I turned twelve

she left this life and moved on to another realm

and now I believe that her leaving

was part of the plan

that she was giving me such a love

letting go of my hand

And there's love and compassion everywhere I go

through illusions of sorrow and pain I somehow know

and sometimes when I wonder

just why I've been born

I know that love has something to do

with my path on earth

And so it goes and round and round we go

The Splendor of each life

touches more than we know

through a simple sigh, sometimes when we cry

and when I close my eyes ~ I know love never dies

And there's love and compassion everywhere I go

through illusions of sorrow and pain

I somehow know

and sometimes when I wonder

just why I've been born

I know that love has something to do

with my path on earth

place of my birth

AMY HINDMAN

SINGER/SONGWRITER

http://www.amyhindman.com

To purchase CD's or books, go to

http://www.amyhindman.com/music.html
http://www.amyhindman.com/books.html

Music also available on iTunes, and CD Baby

To review this book, please go to:

https://www.amazon.com/default/e/B01M1353ON

Songwriting Awards

Puget Symphony

"Best Song Winner"

NW Regional Songwriting Contest

1982

~

Gandhi and King: Becoming the Dream

"Honorable Mention"

Song of the Year 2012

Worldwide Songwriting Competition

~

Seattle Blues / Island Hues

"Semi-Finalist" Award

Song of the Year 2013

Worldwide Songwriting Competition

In My Waking Dream

Song of the Year 2012

Worldwide Songwriting Competition

~

Song of the Earth

"Runner Up Award"

Song of the Year 2017

Worldwide Songwriting Competition

~

A Prayer

"Semi-Finalist" Award

Song of the Year 2018

Worldwide Songwriting Competition

"Her voice is so clear"

Burl Ives

"Her music reflects her influences . . .
James Taylor, Joni Mitchell, The Beatles.
Strong musicians, but moreover
strong songwriters. This describes Amy's music to a tee."

IMPS Journal ~ Independent Music Producers Syndicate

"Throughout time, the voices of the muses
have driven humans to raise their voices in song.
Passion for life has guided artists and visionaries
to create their dreams for everyone to share.
Amy Hindman has added her voice to those who
envision a better future for humankind
and all of our Earth Mother's children.
May these songs touch each of your hearts as well."

Jamie Sams, Author of *Medicine Cards*

www.ingramcontent.com/pod-product-compliance
Lightning Source LLC
Chambersburg PA
CBHW071607040426
42452CB00008B/1273